EMMANUEL JOSEPH

The Crypto Commonwealth, How Billionaires Are Rewriting the Rules of Countries and Influence

Copyright © 2025 by Emmanuel Joseph

All rights reserved. No part of this publication may be reproduced, stored or transmitted in any form or by any means, electronic, mechanical, photocopying, recording, scanning, or otherwise without written permission from the publisher. It is illegal to copy this book, post it to a website, or distribute it by any other means without permission.

First edition

*This book was professionally typeset on Reedsy.
Find out more at reedsy.com*

Contents

1	Chapter 1: The Rise of Digital Fortunes	1
2	Chapter 2: The Decentralized Utopia	3
3	Chapter 3: The New Power Brokers	5
4	Chapter 4: The Ethics of Crypto Wealth	7
5	Chapter 5: The Future of National Economies	9
6	Chapter 6: The Social Impact of Crypto Wealth	11
7	Chapter 7: The Role of Philanthropy in the Crypto Era	13
8	Chapter 8: The Cultural Influence of Crypto Billionaires	15
9	Chapter 9: The Environmental Impact of Crypto Wealth	17
10	Chapter 10: The Intersection of Technology and Society	19
11	Chapter 11: The Impact on Global Governance	21
12	Chapter 12: The Evolution of Financial Systems	23
13	Chapter 13: The Role of Education in the Crypto Era	25
14	Chapter 14: The Future of Work in a Decentralized World	27
15	Chapter 15: The Global Impact of Crypto Philanthropy	29
16	Chapter 16: The Challenges and Opportunities of Crypto...	31
17	Chapter 17: The Future of the Crypto Commonwealth	33

1

Chapter 1: The Rise of Digital Fortunes

With the advent of blockchain technology and the meteoric rise of cryptocurrencies, traditional economic paradigms have been disrupted. The allure of decentralized finance has attracted a new generation of billionaires who see an opportunity to reshape the world's financial landscape. These trailblazers, armed with vast digital fortunes, are challenging the status quo and redefining the concept of wealth and power in the modern era.

The emergence of Bitcoin in 2009 marked the beginning of a new financial revolution. As its value soared, so did the interest of tech-savvy entrepreneurs and investors. They recognized the potential of this digital currency to transcend borders and bypass traditional banking systems. These early adopters, now billionaires, leveraged their newfound wealth to influence global economic policies and forge new alliances.

As the crypto market expanded, so did the number of billionaires who made their fortunes through innovative ventures and strategic investments. These individuals, often dubbed "crypto kings and queens," have become influential figures in politics, philanthropy, and social movements. Their vast resources and forward-thinking mindset have enabled them to challenge established norms and champion causes that align with their vision of a decentralized world.

The unprecedented rise of digital fortunes has also sparked debates about the ethical implications of such immense wealth. Critics argue that the concentration of power in the hands of a few could lead to a new form of digital oligarchy, while proponents believe that these billionaires have the potential to drive positive change and promote financial inclusion on a global scale.

2

Chapter 2: The Decentralized Utopia

The vision of a decentralized utopia is a core belief among crypto billionaires. They envision a world where power is distributed among individuals rather than concentrated in the hands of governments and corporations. This chapter explores how these billionaires are working to create a more equitable society through blockchain technology and decentralized finance.

Decentralized finance (DeFi) has emerged as a powerful tool for disrupting traditional financial systems. By leveraging blockchain technology, DeFi platforms offer financial services such as lending, borrowing, and trading without the need for intermediaries. This has empowered individuals to take control of their financial future and has given rise to a new wave of innovation in the financial sector.

Crypto billionaires are at the forefront of this movement, investing in projects that promote financial inclusion and empower marginalized communities. Through their philanthropic efforts, they are funding initiatives that provide access to education, healthcare, and basic necessities in underserved regions. Their goal is to create a world where everyone has the opportunity to thrive, regardless of their socio-economic background.

However, the path to a decentralized utopia is not without challenges. The regulatory landscape is constantly evolving, and governments around the world are grappling with how to balance innovation with consumer protection. Crypto billionaires must navigate this complex environment while staying true to their vision of a decentralized future.

3

Chapter 3: The New Power Brokers

As crypto billionaires amass wealth and influence, they are becoming the new power brokers in global politics. This chapter examines how they are leveraging their resources to shape policy, lobby for favorable regulations, and support political candidates who align with their vision.

The influence of crypto billionaires extends beyond the financial realm. They are using their wealth to fund think tanks, research institutions, and advocacy groups that promote policies favorable to the growth of blockchain technology and cryptocurrencies. By doing so, they are helping to shape the regulatory environment and ensure that the interests of the crypto community are represented.

In addition to lobbying efforts, crypto billionaires are also supporting political candidates who share their vision of a decentralized world. Through campaign contributions and strategic partnerships, they are helping to elect leaders who understand the potential of blockchain technology and are willing to champion its adoption. This has led to a growing presence of crypto-friendly politicians in governments around the world.

However, the growing influence of crypto billionaires in politics has also raised concerns about the potential for corruption and the erosion of democratic processes. Critics argue that the concentration of power in the hands of a few wealthy individuals could undermine the principles of democracy and lead to a new form of digital feudalism.

4

Chapter 4: The Ethics of Crypto Wealth

The rapid rise of crypto billionaires has sparked a debate about the ethics of wealth accumulation in the digital age. This chapter explores the moral and ethical considerations surrounding the vast fortunes amassed through cryptocurrencies and the impact of this wealth on society.

One of the primary ethical concerns is the environmental impact of cryptocurrency mining. The energy-intensive process of mining cryptocurrencies, particularly Bitcoin, has led to significant carbon emissions and environmental degradation. Crypto billionaires are increasingly aware of this issue and are investing in sustainable mining practices and renewable energy sources to mitigate their environmental footprint.

Another ethical consideration is the potential for wealth inequality in the crypto space. While cryptocurrencies have the potential to democratize finance, the reality is that a small number of individuals hold a significant portion of the total market capitalization. This concentration of wealth has led to concerns about the creation of a new digital aristocracy that could perpetuate existing social inequalities.

Crypto billionaires are also grappling with the ethical implications of their influence on global economic policies. While their philanthropic efforts and investments in social causes are commendable, there is a fine line between using wealth for good and exerting undue influence on policy decisions. The challenge for crypto billionaires is to strike a balance between their desire to drive positive change and the responsibility that comes with their immense wealth.

5

Chapter 5: The Future of National Economies

The rise of crypto billionaires is reshaping national economies and challenging traditional economic models. This chapter examines how the growing influence of these digital magnates is impacting global trade, monetary policy, and economic development.

Cryptocurrencies have the potential to revolutionize global trade by enabling faster, cheaper, and more secure cross-border transactions. Crypto billionaires are investing in projects that facilitate international trade and promote economic growth in developing countries. By leveraging blockchain technology, these projects aim to reduce the barriers to entry for small businesses and create new opportunities for economic development.

The influence of crypto billionaires is also being felt in the realm of monetary policy. Central banks around the world are exploring the potential of central bank digital currencies (CBDCs) as a response to the growing popularity of cryptocurrencies. Crypto billionaires are playing a key role in shaping the development and implementation of these digital currencies, providing valuable insights and expertise to policymakers.

However, the rise of crypto billionaires is also posing challenges for traditional economic models. The decentralized nature of cryptocurrencies makes it difficult for governments to regulate and control their use, leading to concerns about financial stability and the potential for money laundering and other illicit activities. Policymakers must find a way to balance innovation with consumer protection and ensure that the benefits of cryptocurrencies are accessible to all.

6

Chapter 6: The Social Impact of Crypto Wealth

The immense wealth accumulated by crypto billionaires has the potential to drive significant social change. This chapter explores the ways in which these individuals are using their resources to address pressing social issues and promote social justice.

Crypto billionaires are increasingly leveraging their wealth to fund initiatives that address social issues such as poverty, education, and healthcare. Through philanthropic efforts and strategic investments, they are supporting projects that aim to improve the quality of life for marginalized communities and promote social justice. Their goal is to create a more equitable society where everyone has the opportunity to succeed.

One of the key areas where crypto billionaires are making a difference is in financial inclusion. By investing in blockchain-based financial services, they are providing access to banking and financial products for underserved populations. This has the potential to lift millions of people out of poverty and create new economic opportunities in developing countries.

However, the social impact of crypto wealth is not without its challenges. The rapid rise of crypto billionaires has also led to concerns about the potential for wealth inequality and the concentration of power in the hands of a few individuals. Critics argue that the benefits of cryptocurrencies may not be evenly distributed and that the new digital aristocracy could perpetuate existing social inequalities.

7

Chapter 7: The Role of Philanthropy in the Crypto Era

Philanthropy has long been a way for the wealthy to give back to society, and crypto billionaires are no exception. This chapter examines how these digital magnates are using their wealth to fund charitable initiatives and drive positive change.

Crypto billionaires are leveraging their resources to support a wide range of philanthropic initiatives. From funding educational programs to providing disaster relief, they are using their wealth to make a meaningful impact on society. Their philanthropic efforts are often focused on projects that align with their vision of a decentralized world and promote financial inclusion, social justice, and environmental sustainability.

One of the key advantages of crypto philanthropy is the ability to leverage blockchain technology for greater transparency and accountability. By using blockchain-based platforms, crypto billionaires can track the flow of funds and ensure that their donations are being used effectively. This has the potential to revolutionize the way philanthropy is conducted and create a new standard for transparency in charitable giving.

However, the rise of crypto philanthropy also raises important questions about the role of the wealthy in driving social change. While the philanthropic efforts of crypto billionaires are commendable, there is a fine line between using wealth for good and exerting undue influence on social and political issues. The challenge for crypto billionaires is to strike a balance between their desire to drive positive change and the responsibility that comes with their immense wealth.

8

Chapter 8: The Cultural Influence of Crypto Billionaires

The influence of crypto billionaires extends beyond the financial realm and into the world of culture and entertainment. This chapter explores how these digital magnates are shaping cultural trends and redefining the boundaries of art and media.

Crypto billionaires are increasingly investing in cultural and entertainment projects, from funding film productions to supporting contemporary art exhibitions. Their involvement in the cultural sector is driven by a desire to promote innovative and cutting-edge ideas that challenge conventional norms. By supporting avant-garde artists and filmmakers, crypto billionaires are helping to shape the cultural landscape and push the boundaries of artistic expression.

Blockchain technology has also made its way into the art world, with the rise of non-fungible tokens (NFTs) revolutionizing the way art is bought, sold, and owned. Crypto billionaires are at the forefront of this movement, investing in NFT platforms and purchasing digital art pieces for millions of dollars. This has not only provided artists with new revenue streams but has also democratized access to art, allowing collectors from around the world to participate in the market.

The cultural influence of crypto billionaires extends to the media industry as well. By funding independent news organizations and digital media platforms, they are challenging traditional media conglomerates and promoting diverse voices and perspectives. This has led to a more pluralistic media landscape where alternative viewpoints can thrive and reach a global audience.

However, the growing influence of crypto billionaires in culture and media has also sparked debates about the potential for cultural homogenization and the commodification of art. Critics argue that the immense financial power of these individuals could lead to a concentration of cultural production in the hands of a few, potentially stifling creativity and innovation.

9

Chapter 9: The Environmental Impact of Crypto Wealth

The environmental impact of cryptocurrency mining has become a significant concern as the industry continues to grow. This chapter delves into the environmental challenges associated with crypto wealth and the efforts being made by crypto billionaires to mitigate their ecological footprint.

Cryptocurrency mining is an energy-intensive process that requires vast amounts of electricity, often generated from fossil fuels. The carbon footprint of Bitcoin mining, in particular, has drawn criticism from environmentalists and policymakers alike. Crypto billionaires are increasingly aware of the need to address these concerns and are investing in sustainable mining practices and renewable energy sources to reduce their environmental impact.

One of the key initiatives in this regard is the development of green mining technologies that use energy-efficient algorithms and hardware. By adopting these innovations, crypto billionaires aim to minimize the environmental impact of mining operations and promote the use of clean energy in the industry. Additionally, some crypto billionaires are funding research and development projects focused on creating more sustainable blockchain solutions.

Beyond mining, crypto billionaires are also investing in environmental conservation efforts. Through philanthropic initiatives and strategic partnerships, they are supporting projects that aim to protect natural habitats, combat climate change, and promote sustainable development. These efforts reflect their commitment to using their wealth for positive environmental impact and ensuring that the benefits of cryptocurrencies are realized in an ecologically responsible manner.

However, the challenge of balancing innovation with sustainability remains a complex issue. While crypto billionaires are making strides in reducing the environmental impact of their activities, there is still much work to be done to ensure that the industry as a whole operates in an environmentally sustainable manner.

10

Chapter 10: The Intersection of Technology and Society

The influence of crypto billionaires extends beyond finance and into the realm of technology and society. This chapter explores how these digital magnates are shaping the future of technology and its impact on society.

Blockchain technology is at the heart of the crypto revolution, and crypto billionaires are investing heavily in its development and adoption. By funding startups and research initiatives, they are driving innovation in areas such as supply chain management, healthcare, and cybersecurity. These investments are not only transforming industries but also creating new opportunities for economic growth and social progress.

The integration of blockchain technology into everyday life is also changing the way people interact with technology. Crypto billionaires are supporting projects that aim to create more secure and transparent systems for data management, identity verification, and digital transactions. This has the potential to enhance privacy, reduce fraud, and empower individuals to take control of their personal information.

However, the rapid pace of technological advancement also raises important ethical and societal questions. The use of blockchain technology in areas such as surveillance and law enforcement has sparked debates about privacy and civil liberties. Crypto billionaires must navigate these complex issues and ensure that their investments in technology are aligned with ethical principles and societal values.

In addition to their investments in technology, crypto billionaires are also leveraging their influence to promote digital literacy and education. By funding initiatives that provide access to digital skills training and education, they are helping to bridge the digital divide and create a more inclusive digital society.

11

Chapter 11: The Impact on Global Governance

The rise of crypto billionaires is reshaping the landscape of global governance and challenging traditional power structures. This chapter examines how these digital magnates are influencing international relations and the role of governments in the crypto era.

Cryptocurrencies operate on a global scale, transcending national borders and traditional regulatory frameworks. This has created a new set of challenges for governments and international organizations as they seek to navigate the complex and rapidly evolving world of digital finance. Crypto billionaires are playing a key role in shaping the global governance of cryptocurrencies by participating in international forums and advocating for policies that promote innovation and financial inclusion.

One of the key areas where crypto billionaires are making an impact is in the development of global standards for blockchain technology and digital assets. By collaborating with policymakers, regulators, and industry stakeholders, they are helping to create a regulatory environment that balances innovation with consumer protection. This has the potential to foster greater trust and stability in the global crypto market.

The influence of crypto billionaires in global governance is also evident in their support for initiatives that promote international cooperation and development. Through philanthropic efforts and strategic investments, they are funding projects that address global challenges such as poverty, healthcare, and climate change. Their goal is to create a more interconnected and resilient world where the benefits of cryptocurrencies are accessible to all.

However, the growing influence of crypto billionaires in global governance has also raised concerns about the potential for conflicts of interest and the erosion of democratic processes. Critics argue that the concentration of power in the hands of a few wealthy individuals could undermine the principles of transparency and accountability in international relations.

12

Chapter 12: The Evolution of Financial Systems

The rise of crypto billionaires is driving the evolution of financial systems and challenging traditional banking models. This chapter explores how these digital magnates are transforming the financial industry and shaping the future of money.

Decentralized finance (DeFi) has emerged as a powerful force for disruption in the financial sector. By leveraging blockchain technology, DeFi platforms offer a wide range of financial services such as lending, borrowing, and trading without the need for intermediaries. Crypto billionaires are at the forefront of this movement, investing in DeFi projects and promoting the adoption of decentralized financial solutions.

The impact of DeFi on traditional banking models is profound. By removing the need for intermediaries, DeFi platforms have the potential to reduce costs, increase efficiency, and enhance financial inclusion. Crypto billionaires are driving this transformation by funding startups and research initiatives that aim to create more accessible and user-friendly financial services.

In addition to DeFi, crypto billionaires are also exploring the potential of central bank digital currencies (CBDCs) as a means of modernizing the financial system. By collaborating with central banks and policymakers, they are helping to shape the development and implementation of CBDCs. This has the potential to create a more stable and secure financial system that leverages the benefits of blockchain technology.

However, the rapid evolution of financial systems also raises important regulatory and security challenges. The decentralized nature of cryptocurrencies and DeFi platforms makes it difficult for governments to regulate and control their use, leading to concerns about financial stability and the potential for illicit activities. Crypto billionaires must navigate this complex regulatory landscape while promoting innovation and ensuring the security and integrity of the financial system.

13

Chapter 13: The Role of Education in the Crypto Era

Education is a key factor in the growth and development of the crypto industry. This chapter examines how crypto billionaires are investing in education and promoting digital literacy to ensure the future success of the crypto ecosystem.

Crypto billionaires recognize the importance of education in driving innovation and adoption in the crypto space. By funding educational programs and initiatives, they are helping to create a knowledgeable and skilled workforce that can support the growth of the industry. These efforts include sponsoring scholarships, funding research projects, and supporting blockchain education programs at universities and institutions around the world.

One of the key areas of focus for crypto billionaires is promoting digital literacy and financial education. By providing access to training and resources, they are helping individuals understand the potential of blockchain technology and cryptocurrencies. This has the potential to empower individuals to take control of their financial future and participate in the digital economy.

In addition to formal education programs, crypto billionaires are also leveraging online platforms and social media to spread awareness and knowledge about cryptocurrencies. By creating educational content and engaging with the community, they are helping to demystify the technology and promote its adoption among a wider audience.

However, the challenge of educating the public about cryptocurrencies is not without its obstacles. The rapid pace of technological advancement and the complexity of blockchain technology can make it difficult for individuals to keep up with the latest developments. Crypto billionaires must find innovative ways to make education more accessible and engaging to ensure that everyone has the opportunity to benefit from the digital revolution.

14

Chapter 14: The Future of Work in a Decentralized World

The rise of crypto billionaires is transforming the future of work and creating new opportunities in the digital economy. This chapter explores how these digital magnates are shaping the future of employment and the impact of blockchain technology on the job market.

Blockchain technology is creating new opportunities for remote work and decentralized organizations. Crypto billionaires are investing in projects that leverage blockchain to create more flexible and efficient work environments. By supporting decentralized autonomous organizations (DAOs), they are promoting a new model of governance and collaboration that empowers individuals to work on their own terms.

The impact of blockchain technology on the job market is also creating new career opportunities in areas such as software development, cybersecurity, and blockchain consulting. Crypto billionaires are investing in education and training programs to equip individuals with the skills needed to thrive in the digital economy. These efforts are helping to create a new generation of workers who are proficient in blockchain technology and capable of driving innovation in the industry.

Decentralized work models are also changing the way people think about employment and career development. By enabling remote work and flexible work arrangements, blockchain technology is empowering individuals to take control of their careers and pursue opportunities that align with their interests and values. This has the potential to create a more inclusive and diverse workforce where individuals have the freedom to work on their own terms.

However, the transition to a decentralized work environment also presents challenges. The lack of traditional employment structures and job security can create uncertainty for workers and raise questions about the future of labor rights and protections. Crypto billionaires must navigate these complex issues and find ways to ensure that the benefits of decentralized work are accessible to all.

In addition to creating new opportunities, the rise of crypto billionaires is also driving innovation in workplace technology. By investing in blockchain-based solutions for project management, collaboration, and communication, they are helping to create more efficient and productive work environments. These innovations have the potential to transform the way people work and create new possibilities for collaboration and creativity.

15

Chapter 15: The Global Impact of Crypto Philanthropy

Crypto billionaires are using their wealth to address global challenges and promote social progress. This chapter examines the impact of crypto philanthropy on issues such as poverty, healthcare, and education, and the role of crypto billionaires in driving positive change.

Crypto philanthropy has the potential to revolutionize the way charitable giving is conducted. By leveraging blockchain technology, crypto billionaires can ensure greater transparency and accountability in their philanthropic efforts. This has the potential to create a new standard for charitable giving and promote greater trust and confidence in the nonprofit sector.

One of the key areas where crypto philanthropy is making a difference is in the fight against poverty. Crypto billionaires are funding initiatives that provide access to financial services, education, and healthcare for underserved populations. These efforts are helping to create new economic opportunities and improve the quality of life for individuals and communities around the world.

In the realm of healthcare, crypto billionaires are supporting projects that aim to improve access to medical care and promote public health. By funding research and development initiatives, they are helping to advance medical innovation and create new treatments for diseases. Their philanthropic efforts are also focused on addressing global health challenges such as pandemics and improving healthcare infrastructure in developing countries.

Education is another key focus area for crypto philanthropy. By investing in educational programs and initiatives, crypto billionaires are helping to create a more knowledgeable and skilled workforce. These efforts include funding scholarships, supporting research projects, and promoting digital literacy. By providing access to education and training, crypto billionaires are empowering individuals to achieve their full potential and contribute to the growth of the digital economy.

16

Chapter 16: The Challenges and Opportunities of Crypto Regulation

The rise of crypto billionaires has brought new challenges and opportunities for regulators and policymakers. This chapter explores the regulatory landscape of the crypto industry and the efforts of crypto billionaires to navigate and shape it.

The decentralized nature of cryptocurrencies presents unique challenges for regulators. Traditional regulatory frameworks are often ill-equipped to address the complexities of digital finance and the rapid pace of technological innovation. Crypto billionaires are playing a key role in shaping the regulatory environment by advocating for policies that promote innovation and protect consumers.

One of the key challenges for regulators is balancing innovation with consumer protection. While cryptocurrencies offer numerous benefits, they also present risks such as fraud, money laundering, and cybersecurity threats. Crypto billionaires are working with regulators to develop frameworks that address these risks while promoting the growth of the industry.

The global nature of cryptocurrencies also complicates regulatory efforts. Different countries have adopted varying approaches to regulating digital assets, leading to a fragmented regulatory landscape. Crypto billionaires are advocating for greater international cooperation and harmonization of regulations to create a more consistent and predictable environment for the crypto industry.

Despite the challenges, the evolving regulatory landscape also presents opportunities for innovation and growth. By working with regulators, crypto billionaires can help shape policies that support the development of blockchain technology and promote financial inclusion. This has the potential to create a more stable and secure crypto market and unlock new opportunities for economic growth.

17

Chapter 17: The Future of the Crypto Commonwealth

The rise of crypto billionaires is reshaping the world in profound ways. This final chapter explores the future of the crypto commonwealth and the potential for cryptocurrencies to transform global finance, governance, and society.

The potential of cryptocurrencies to create a more decentralized and equitable world is vast. Crypto billionaires are leading the charge in promoting financial inclusion, driving innovation, and addressing global challenges. Their efforts are helping to create a new paradigm for wealth and power, where individuals have greater control over their financial future and the benefits of digital technology are accessible to all.

The future of the crypto commonwealth will be shaped by the continued development and adoption of blockchain technology. As the technology evolves, new use cases and applications will emerge, further transforming industries and creating new opportunities for economic growth. Crypto billionaires will play a crucial role in driving this innovation and ensuring that the benefits of blockchain technology are realized on a global scale.

However, the future of the crypto commonwealth also hinges on the ability to address the challenges and risks associated with digital finance. Issues such as regulatory compliance, cybersecurity, and environmental sustainability must be addressed to ensure the long-term success and stability of the crypto industry. Crypto billionaires, regulators, and industry stakeholders must work together to navigate these challenges and create a secure and sustainable future for the crypto commonwealth.

In conclusion, the rise of crypto billionaires is rewriting the rules of countries and influence. Their immense wealth and influence are driving significant changes in global finance, governance, and society. As we look to the future, the crypto commonwealth holds the promise of a more decentralized, inclusive, and innovative world. The journey ahead is filled with challenges and opportunities, and the collective efforts of crypto billionaires and the global community will shape the future of this dynamic and transformative movement.

The Crypto Commonwealth: How Billionaires Are Rewriting the Rules of Countries and Influence

In "The Crypto Commonwealth: How Billionaires Are Rewriting the Rules of Countries and Influence," dive into the electrifying world of cryptocurrency magnates who are reshaping the very fabric of our global society. This thought-provoking book explores how these digital titans, armed with unprecedented wealth and technological prowess, are challenging traditional power structures and forging a new path toward a decentralized future.

Through seventeen meticulously crafted chapters, readers will embark on a journey that uncovers the rise of digital fortunes, the vision of a decentralized utopia, and the ethical considerations of immense crypto wealth. The book delves into the intricate dynamics of crypto billionaires as new power brokers in global politics, their philanthropic efforts, and their influence on cultural trends, national economies, and global governance.

"The Crypto Commonwealth" offers a comprehensive look at the social, environmental, and technological impact of crypto wealth, shedding light on how these trailblazers are driving innovation, promoting financial inclusion, and addressing global challenges. From the evolution of financial systems to the future of work in a decentralized world, this book provides a visionary perspective on the transformative power of blockchain technology.

Join us as we explore the profound implications of the crypto revolution

CHAPTER 17: THE FUTURE OF THE CRYPTO COMMONWEALTH

and the pivotal role of billionaires in shaping a more inclusive, equitable, and sustainable world. Whether you're a crypto enthusiast, a curious observer, or a skeptic, "The Crypto Commonwealth" will leave you with a deeper understanding of the dynamic forces at play in our rapidly changing world.

www.ingramcontent.com/pod-product-compliance
Lightning Source LLC
Chambersburg PA
CBHW060034040426
42333CB00042B/2447